Con

Corton Primary School, Corton

Theo Chenery (6)	1
Kaulton Hudson (7)	2
Annabelle Jayne Jacobs (6)	3
Jake Robinson (6), River, Blake Jessup (5) & Ellie Shave (5)	4
Amelie Thurston (5)	5
Freddie Poppy (5)	6
Archie Francis (6)	7
Cole Highfield (6)	8
Charlie Finch (5)	9
Isaac Bailey (5)	10

Eynsham Community Primary School, Eynsham

Lizzie Crowe (5)	11
Rayan Al Faqih (5)	12
Luke Besnard (5)	13
Delilah Holden (5)	14
Luke Owen (5)	15
Iness Jennings (5)	16
Polly Aspinall (6)	17
Sophie Cockwell (5)	18
Isla Kilby (5)	19
Weronika Szewczyk (5)	20
Mason Johnson-Macburnie (6)	21
Hamish Boyce (5)	22
Edith Schlingloff (5), Yasin Saad (6), James Ayres (5), Amber Grant (5), Tshiamo & Luca Basterfield (6)	23
James Everist (5)	24

Fairfield Primary School, South Wigston

Tyler Farren (6)	25
Leo Hanes (6)	26
Thomas Armstrong (6)	27
Keilah-Zoey Nkwinkeh (6)	28
Coco-Starr Mayfield (6)	29
Lily Endall (6)	30
L'naie Barratt (6)	31
Oliver Lambert (6)	32
Frankie Currie (6)	33
Erin Sawyers-Short (6)	34
Freddie Marski (6)	35
Dougie Waters (6)	36
Marika Bis (6)	37
Rome Diaper (6)	38
Sayab Birkin (7)	39
Nancy Orme (6)	40
Lacie Siddon (6)	41
Harry Fletcher (7)	42
Grace Louch (6)	43
Zak Clarke (6)	44
Warren Middleton (6)	45
Cooper Carey (6)	46

Hollesley Primary School, Hollesley

Nathaniel Bailey (6)	47
Lilly Read (6)	48
Amelia Larcombe (5)	49
Ettie Curtis (6)	50
Florence Backhouse (6)	51
Sam Hague (7)	52
Oliver Johnson (7)	53

Constance Sibbring (6) 54
Logan Sones (6) 55
Mason Craig (6) 56
Isla McCann (5) 57
Luisana Conde-Harvey (5) 58
Huw Butler (5) 59
Flynn Tyler-Smith (6) 60
Daniel Collins (6) 61
Leo O'Hara (6) 62

Kennoway Primary School, Kennoway

Lucy Anna Burns (7) 63
Reese Dryden (7) 64
Nathan Scobie (7) 65
Lily McDougall (7) 66
Madison Mackenzie (7) 67
Shelby-Leigh Handley- 68
Shinnie (7)
Sam George Sutherland (7) 69
Annalise Allan (7) 70
Faith Raggett (7) 71
Paige Small (8) 72
Kai Harron (7) 73
Daimon Taylor (7) 74
Kaitlyn Wilson (7) 75
Dani Curran (7) 76
Zak Paul (7) 77
Mason Little (7) 78
Oban Cation (7) 79
Ellie Blount (7) 80
Alexis Hay (7) 81
Kelvin Mackenzie (7) 82
Logan Simpson (7) 83
Blake Curran (7) 84
Jayden Mackie (7) 85

Kirkcaldy West Primary School, Kirkcaldy

Jagoda Sieklinska (7) 86
Martyna Zabek (7) 87
Oliver Scott (7) 88
Luka Indopoulous (7) 89
Nikita Farmer (7) 90
Hope Lazmirski (7) 91
Elsa Venters (7) 92
Arabella Blacklaws (7) 93
Harvey Deacon (7) 94
Lily Meacher (7) 95
Scarlett Stewart (7) 96
Jack Fairfull (7) 97
Stephen Chaplin (7) 98
Indie McQuade (7) 99
Kuba Jakubaszek (7) 100
Rory Seal (7) 101

Notting Hill & Ealing Junior School, Ealing

Cissie Bootman (6) 102
Jemima Omiyale (5) 103
Daria Coulon (5) 104
Himari Shinno (5) 105
Ārya Sharma (6) 106
Eden Lily Gambling (7) 107
Hannah Clough (6) 108
Anaahi Shah (6) 109
Cindy Yu (6) 110
Mira Bachir (5) 111
Umi Cook Kurihara (5) 112
Yvie Huang (6) 113
Isobel MacDougall (6) 114
Laranya Ryatt (6) 115
Savannah McDowell (6) 116
Olivia Qin (5) 117
Ines Coulter (6) 118
Lyla Peat (6) 119
Rishita Sharma (5) 120
Emilia Priestley (6) 121
Charlotte Gilbert (6) 122

AN ACROSTIC FOR YOU

Little Gems

Edited By Roseanna Caswell

First published in Great Britain in 2021 by:

Young Writers
Remus House
Coltsfoot Drive
Peterborough
PE2 9BF
Telephone: 01733 890066
Website: www.youngwriters.co.uk

Printed and bound in the UK by BookPrintingUK
Website: www.bookprintinguk.com
YB0454N

Foreword

Dear Reader,

Welcome to a fun-filled book of acrostic poems!

Here at Young Writers, we are delighted to introduce our new poetry competition for pupils aged 5-7 years, An Acrostic For You. Acrostic poems are an enjoyable way to introduce pupils to the world of poetry and allow the young writers to open their imaginations to a range of topics of their choice. The engaging worksheets allowed even the youngest (or most reluctant) of writers to create a poem using the acrostic technique, and with that, encouraged them to include other literary techniques such as similes and description. Here at Young Writers we are passionate about introducing the love and art of creative writing to the next generation and we love being a part of their journey.

From family to teachers, from pets to popstars, these pupils have shaped and crafted their ideas brilliantly, showcasing their budding creativity as they celebrate the people that are important to them. More than ever it's important to show our appreciation to the people who do so much for us, and these young poets are a shining example of how to do just that. We hope you will delight in these poems as much as we have.

Zoe Pole (6)	123	Miryam Khan (16)	159
Jasmine Takhar (6)	124	Eva Hopkins (11)	160
Aadhya Parikh (6)	125	Shea Hegarty (12)	161
Hettie Heppenstall (6)	126	Sean Nyathi (12)	162
Millie Milne (6)	127		
Millie Lockett-Boyle (6)	128		
Nikita Pillai (7)	129		
Anika Sangwaiya (5)	130		
Ottilie Coman (6)	131		
Lubna Al-Jibouri (6)	132		
Emma Louise Melikian (6)	133		
Josie Johnstone (5)	134		
Blythe Tyler (5)	135		
Aanya Saboo (6)	136		
Mina Burge (5)	137		

Rettendon Primary School, Rettendon Common

Freddie Forecast (6)	138
Annabelle Morter (6)	139
Charlie De-Beger (5)	140
Joseph Watts (6)	141
Ella Goodacre (5)	142
Elliott Bray (5)	143
Henry Sharp (5)	144
Rosie Kemp (5)	145
Grace Francks (5)	146
Jai Gill (5)	147
Isabelle Wang (5)	148
Macy Tinton (5)	149
Archie West (5)	150
Beau Ayliffe (6)	151
John James Hiscott (6)	152
Oliver Medlock (5)	153
Nathan McCreadie (5)	154

The Coppice School, Bamber Bridge

Paul Heary (17)	155
Lexi Coulton (12)	156
Emily Holt (12)	157
Josh Ormson (16)	158

The
Poems

Robot

R usty in the autumn rain

O peration on his heart

B luebird landed on the shoulders

O ver the mountains

T icklish inside the robot heart.

Theo Chenery (6)

Corton Primary School, Corton

Robot

R usting in the rain
O peration on his heart
B lizzard is foggy
O range is the robot
T icklish in the cold.

Kaulton Hudson (7)

Corton Primary School, Corton

Robot

R obot is rusting

O nly one alone

B lizzard and cold

O ver excited

T ime to say goodbye, Bluebird.

Annabelle Jayne Jacobs (6)

Corton Primary School, Corton

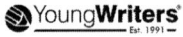

Robot

R usty

O peration on his heart

B ig belly

O n his shoulder

T he bluebird landed. He was excited.

Jake Robinson (6), River, Blake Jessup (5) & Ellie Shave (5)

Corton Primary School, Corton

Robot

R ain, rusty and cold

O ver the mountains

B luebird

O utside it is cold

T op of the mountains.

Amelie Thurston (5)
Corton Primary School, Corton

Robot

R usting in the rain

O ver excited when the bluebird was singing

B lizzard

O utside

T icklish.

Freddie Poppy (5)
Corton Primary School, Corton

Robot

R obot is hot

O ver the mountain

B luebird

O ver the mountain

T he robot has a broken heart.

Archie Francis (6)

Corton Primary School, Corton

Robot

R obot is cold
O ld robot
B luebird is beautiful
O ff the sun
T he robot is sad.

Cole Highfield (6)
Corton Primary School, Corton

Robot

R usting

O ld robot

B luebird

O ver the mountain

T he excited bird.

Charlie Finch (5)

Corton Primary School, Corton

Robot

R usty

O range

B lizzard

O peration

T icklish.

Isaac Bailey (5)

Corton Primary School, Corton

Playing With Friends

F riendly to your friends

R espect your friends

I nvite your friends to a party

E xcited your friends are coming

N ow your friends know what to do

D on't forget your friends

S afe with your friends

H ealthy with your friends

I mpress your friends

P roud of your friends.

Lizzie Crowe (5)

Eynsham Community Primary School, Eynsham

Courageous

C ount

O n me

U s being afraid of nothing.

R eady so you won't be afraid,

A fraid of nothing you should be.

G reat is to be brave.

E ars help you hear so you won't be scared.

O kay is sometimes to be scared.

U s being brave,

S orry for being scared sometimes.

Rayan Al Faqih (5)

Eynsham Community Primary School, Eynsham

Friendship

F riends are together
R espectful to each other
I like football
E verybody likes each other
N o fighting
D inosaur games are fun
S hare each other's toys
H appy together
I win the race
P eas are great for me.

Luke Besnard (5)
Eynsham Community Primary School, Eynsham

Friends Love

F riends are forever
R unning to play with you
I am loving you
E xcellent friend
N o hurting
D on't let down others
S hare your friends
H appy for you
I love my friends in my heart
P arty in the house.

Delilah Holden (5)
Eynsham Community Primary School, Eynsham

My Friends

F riends forever

R aces are fun

I love my friends

E li and Isla are helpful

N ow I am going to play

D on't bite

S ometimes love school

H appy tears

I ce cream with them

P laying is fun.

Luke Owen (5)

Eynsham Community Primary School, Eynsham

Friendship

F abulous friends
R un together
I like school
E veryone is excited
N ice friends
D o you like playing with me?
S mile at Eli and Isla
H appy with Isla and Eli
I love Alexa
P laying is fun.

Iness Jennings (5)

Eynsham Community Primary School, Eynsham

Sharing

F riends are fun

R unning wildly

I like you

E ach other can play

N ever fall out

D on't forget your friend

S hall we play?

H appy feelings

I love playing with you

P erfect playing.

Polly Aspinall (6)

Eynsham Community Primary School, Eynsham

Caring

F riendship is nice

R unning around

I like football

E xcited to be at school

N o hurting others

D on't push

S mile at them

H amish is nice

I like playing

P lease be nice.

Sophie Cockwell (5)

Eynsham Community Primary School, Eynsham

Friendship

F riends together
R unning outside
I like my friends
E li is my friend
N ice friends
D on't hurt others
S hare games
H appy friends
I ness is my friend
P lay is fun.

Isla Kilby (5)

Eynsham Community Primary School, Eynsham

Time With Friends

F riends are forever
R unning together
I love you so much
E li is my best friend
N icely forever
D oing
S omething
H ugs
I love you
P laying is fun.

Weronika Szewczyk (5)

Eynsham Community Primary School, Eynsham

Friend

F riendship is forever

R eggie is my best friend

I like my friend

E li is nice

N o hurting

D on't let down friends.

Mason Johnson-Macburnie (6)

Eynsham Community Primary School, Eynsham

Caring

F riendship is nice
R eggie is my friend
I love you
E xcited to be here
N ice to meet you
D o you want to be my friend?

Hamish Boyce (5)
Eynsham Community Primary School, Eynsham

Friend

F ootball is fun

R un in the playground

I f we had good friends

E ach take a turn

N ever fear

D on't worry.

Edith Schlingloff (5), Yasin Saad (6), James Ayres (5), Amber Grant (5), Tshiamo & Luca Basterfield (6)
Eynsham Community Primary School, Eynsham

Sharing

F riends are kind

R unning outside

I like playing

E xcited to play

N ice people

D on't play rough.

James Everist (5)

Eynsham Community Primary School, Eynsham

Mr Chatterbox

M r Chatterbox is pink
R eally noisy

C hats all the time
H as a green hat
A lways kind
T alks to all of his friends
T ells lots of stories
E verybody likes him
R arely stops talking
B lah, blah, blah
O n and on and on
X -ray is his favourite word.

Tyler Farren (6)

Fairfield Primary School, South Wigston

Dinosaur

D inosaurs are strong

I love dinosaurs

N ever get too close to a dinosaur

O nce they were alive 66 million years ago

S uper strength to kill other dinosaurs

A t prehistoric times they lived

U nder the sea is where sea monsters lived

R uled the planet.

Leo Hanes (6)

Fairfield Primary School, South Wigston

Animals

A nacondas are poisonous

N o dinosaurs living now

I n the zoo there are seals

M ummy spiders are good at climbing

A black widow spider is yellow with stripes

L ong necks on giraffes

S ome butterflies can fly from England to Spain.

Thomas Armstrong (6)

Fairfield Primary School, South Wigston

Friend

F riends are nice and funny and happy. I don't like

R ude friends. I like nice friends

I am always happy

E verybody is kind, so everybody is happy

N ow everybody can't touch, but we are still having fun

D o I have the best friends?

Keilah-Zoey Nkwinkeh (6)

Fairfield Primary School, South Wigston

Coco-Starr

C oco loves playing
O nce I was little
C aring and kind
O nly scared of the dark

S illy at Nanny's house
T oast is yummy
A lways smiling
R eally good at writing
R ed is my favourite colour.

Coco-Starr Mayfield (6)
Fairfield Primary School, South Wigston

Toothless

T oothless is scary

O utside playing

O utside flying

T oothless' tail is broken

H iccup lets him play

L ove Hiccup

E very day he fights dragons

S illy dragon hunters

S cared of nothing.

Lily Endall (6)

Fairfield Primary School, South Wigston

Fairies

F airies are beautiful

A lways flutter in the night

I n the night, fairies are cuter

R un fairies to your home

I n the night fairies flutter

E very fairy finds their home

S ome fairies are pink.

L'naie Barratt (6)

Fairfield Primary School, South Wigston

Dinosaur

D inosaurs were dangerous
I am small, they were big
N ot going near dinosaurs
O range dinosaurs are big
S illy dinosaurs
A dinosaur is big
U nder the trees
R ex was a big dinosaur.

Oliver Lambert (6)
Fairfield Primary School, South Wigston

Dinosaur

D inosaurs lived 66 million years ago
I like dinosaurs
N o dinosaurs now
O n top of a rock
S urrounded
A dinosaur is big
U ses their claws
R oaring dinosaurs.

Frankie Currie (6)
Fairfield Primary School, South Wigston

Friend

F riendly Lilith plays with me
R eally kind helping the children
I nside we play Shopkins together
E njoy playing at break time
N ever ever nasty
D ifferent in nice ways.

Erin Sawyers-Short (6)

Fairfield Primary School, South Wigston

Hamster

H is name is Oreo

A lways biting the bars

M aking lots of mess

S leeping in his corner

T oys are his favourite

E ating lots of carrots

R unning in his ball.

Freddie Marski (6)
Fairfield Primary School, South Wigston

Rainbow

R ainbows are my favourite
A lways colourful
I like rainbows
N ever change colour
B right orange
O range is in the rainbow
W hat colour is in the rainbow?

Dougie Waters (6)
Fairfield Primary School, South Wigston

School

S chool is the best in the world
C lass is the best place to do work
H appy when I am in school
O ther friends and sharing
O utside is fun
L ove maths and English.

Marika Bis (6)
Fairfield Primary School, South Wigston

Friend

F riend is my dad

R ome is the greatest

I love Anais, she is the greatest

E den is the best

N ever sad with Mum

D ad is the best.

Rome Diaper (6)

Fairfield Primary School, South Wigston

Friend

F unny

R ed is his favourite colour

I love my friend

E xcited to see me

N ever gives up

D oesn't stop being my friend.

Sayab Birkin (7)

Fairfield Primary School, South Wigston

Sister

S he is nice and funny

I love my sister

S he likes to run

T he day I said I love you

E xcited to go out

R un to the house.

Nancy Orme (6)

Fairfield Primary School, South Wigston

Lacie

L ove my trampoline

A lways happy

C hocolate is one of my favourite foods

I like to play with my friends

E ating sweets I love.

Lacie Siddon (6)

Fairfield Primary School, South Wigston

Harry

H arry is cool
A t school I am clever
R abbits are my favourite
R eally like motorbikes
Y ummy tikka masala.

Harry Fletcher (7)
Fairfield Primary School, South Wigston

Daddy

D ad is strong

A mazing Daddy

D addy is brave

D addy fights with me and Brooke

Y oghurt is his favourite.

Grace Louch (6)

Fairfield Primary School, South Wigston

Zak C

Z ak likes bibles
A ll the time I read bibles
K az is my favourite YouTuber

C larke is my last name.

Zak Clarke (6)
Fairfield Primary School, South Wigston

Toby

T oby is kind

O tters he likes

B est big brother

Y oghurt is his favourite.

Warren Middleton (6)

Fairfield Primary School, South Wigston

Cat

C ute and cuddly
A lways wanting snuggles
T hunder is his name.

Cooper Carey (6)
Fairfield Primary School, South Wigston

Mrs Roberts

M rs Roberts help me learn
R eading is something I like
S ums are my favourite thing

R eally love a 'Mrs Roberts' challenge
O n Thursday, we do times tables rock stars
B est lesson is maths
E very day, I practise my times tables
R eally good at them
T he teacher is really kind and beautiful
S he helps me do new things.

Nathaniel Bailey (6)
Hollesley Primary School, Hollesley

Best Friend

B est friend, Taylor
E ager Taylor
S ister Taylor
T all Taylor

F unny Taylor
R eally good Taylor
I love Taylor
E very day, Taylor plays
N ice Taylor
D ancing Taylor.

Lilly Read (6)

Hollesley Primary School, Hollesley

Florence

F lorence is very kind

L ong blonde hair

O ur playtimes are fun

R unning in the playground

E veryone plays

N obody argues

C an you jump?

E very day I play with her.

Amelia Larcombe (5)
Hollesley Primary School, Hollesley

Winnie

W innie is a tortoiseshell and super cute
　I love Winnie very much
N ot a nasty bone in her
N ever hisses or scratches
　I love playing with her
E ttie loves to feed her secret treats.

Ettie Curtis (6)
Hollesley Primary School, Hollesley

Amelia

A melia is good to me
M y friend is always nice
E very day we play on the tyres
L ong play with her beautiful hair
I love when Amelia comes
A melia likes to play with everyone.

Florence Backhouse (6)
Hollesley Primary School, Hollesley

Daddy

D addy helps me do up my laces
A long time ago, Daddy loved his tank
D addy gives the best tickles
D addy even helps people who have Coronavirus
Y esterday, Daddy put on the car telly.

Sam Hague (7)
Hollesley Primary School, Hollesley

My Pet

M y dog, Bailey, chews blue balls
Y ou would love my dog

P eople play with Bailey in the forest
E verybody nearby has met him
T hey all love my brown pet, Bailey.

Oliver Johnson (7)
Hollesley Primary School, Hollesley

Mummy

M y mummy gives the best hugs
U sually, we snuggle on Mummy's bed
M ummy is cuddly and cute
M aking the best apple tarts
Y ou are very happy to be around.

Constance Sibbring (6)

Hollesley Primary School, Hollesley

Uncle

U ncle Bob, he's always making apple pie

N ow he is making cheese pizza

C ould he make meatballs today?

L ove his meatballs

E ating all the meatballs up.

Logan Sones (6)

Hollesley Primary School, Hollesley

Mummy

M y mummy is nice

U sually, she is very kind

M ummy makes the best dinner in the world

M y mummy is the best mummy ever

Y es, she is, we love her.

Mason Craig (6)
Hollesley Primary School, Hollesley

Adam

A dam, you are the best because you let me go on the Xbox

D id you tidy your room? It is usually a mess

A dam, you make me smile

M y brother is the best.

Isla McCann (5)
Hollesley Primary School, Hollesley

Loren

L oren likes to swim in the pool
O n holiday I want to see her
R eally long journey on a plane
E veryone gets tired
N ew Zealand is her home.

Luisana Conde-Harvey (5)
Hollesley Primary School, Hollesley

Mummy

M ummy is a teacher
U sually, she comes home just before bed
M ummy is good at cooking
M akes lovely cakes
Y ummy, they are the best ever.

Huw Butler (5)

Hollesley Primary School, Hollesley

Toby

T oby is seven years old
O ur favourite game is running
B alls with ropes are his favourite to play with
Y ou'll find him in the park.

Flynn Tyler-Smith (6)
Hollesley Primary School, Hollesley

Mummy

M ummy plays

U sually, we play trains

M ummy helps make the train tracks

M y mummy helps me do spellings

Y es, I love Mummy.

Daniel Collins (6)

Hollesley Primary School, Hollesley

Leo

L eo likes to play games like Minecraft
E veryone helps me when I am sad
O n the way to school, I meet friends.

Leo O'Hara (6)

Hollesley Primary School, Hollesley

My Teacher

M arvellous teacher with a good class

R ecommended for giving hard work

S uper Simpson likes his class

I s the best and perfect

M y best teacher ever, he's never grumpy but fabulous

P erfect, happy, incredible

S uperhero Simpson

O n the ball, because he likes football

N ot nippy any day.

Lucy Anna Burns (7)

Kennoway Primary School, Kennoway

Mummy

M y mum is kind and caring
Y esterday, my mum gave me sweets

M e and my mum can't sleep when it is
Christmas
U nicorns my mum likes
M y mum is going to take me to Gran's
M y mum is pretty
Y esterday, she picked me up.

Reese Dryden (7)
Kennoway Primary School, Kennoway

Cute Brother

C onstantly, my brother is so cute
U sually, my brother is cute
T o my brother, I love you
E at more food, brother

J elly is good for you
O ver there, brother
S aw it, brother
H i brother!

Nathan Scobie (7)
Kennoway Primary School, Kennoway

My Friend

K aitlyn loves lollipops
A pples are Kaitlyn's favourite food
I am Kaitlyn's BFF
T alented at dancing
L oves to dance
Y esterday, she had dancing
N ice to me every day.

Lily McDougall (7)
Kennoway Primary School, Kennoway

My Grandad

G reat, he is

R eactions are good

A wesome is my grandad

N ever mean to anyone

D rinks tea all the time

A mazing at watching TV

D iscos he likes.

Madison Mackenzie (7)
Kennoway Primary School, Kennoway

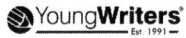

Lacey

L acey likes lollipops

A t school, she plays with boys

C aring about Terri all the time

E very time we go somewhere fun, she gets excited

Y esterday, she had gym.

Shelby-Leigh Handley-Shinnie (7)

Kennoway Primary School, Kennoway

My Mum

A mazing, funny Mum
I Phone is her favourite thing
M um is caring for me
E very day, my mum goes on Gardenscapes
E very morning, my mum drops me off at school.

Sam George Sutherland (7)
Kennoway Primary School, Kennoway

Annalise And Grandad

G ood at thinking
R eally funny
A cool person
N ow he's fun
D id he do the funny stuff?
A mazing Grandad
D o we like? Yes!

Annalise Allan (7)
Kennoway Primary School, Kennoway

My Cousin

C aring in the community
O rganised every day
U nder the world I love her
S uper Lola can help
I love her
N ever mean to anyone.

Faith Raggett (7)
Kennoway Primary School, Kennoway

Best Friend

M illie is so cool
I n my house she is caring
L ikes my dog
L ikes to play
I s my best friend
E ven when I'm grumpy.

Paige Small (8)
Kennoway Primary School, Kennoway

My Mum

M y mum is beautiful
U nderstands, she is good to me
M arvellous Mum, she is pretty
M um, I love you
Y es, she likes unicorns.

Kai Harron (7)
Kennoway Primary School, Kennoway

Best Mum In The World

M y mum lets us have the phone
U nicorns she loves
M y dog snores like my mum
M y mummy is kind
Y es, my mum loves me.

Daimon Taylor (7)
Kennoway Primary School, Kennoway

My Best Friend, Lily

L ovely Lily loves to lick lollipops
I like lily coming to my house
L ily is my BFF
Y ellow is Lily's favourite colour.

Kaitlyn Wilson (7)
Kennoway Primary School, Kennoway

Our NHS

N urses are the best

U norganised at home

R ights and responsibilities

S ensible and sensitive

E ncouraging.

Dani Curran (7)

Kennoway Primary School, Kennoway

Nice Sister

S he is nice

I s caring and kind

S isters are pretty

T o the shop

E mily is nice

R achel is nice.

Zak Paul (7)

Kennoway Primary School, Kennoway

Teacher

T errific

E nergetic

A good teacher

C aring

H appy

E njoys teaching

R espectful.

Mason Little (7)

Kennoway Primary School, Kennoway

My Pet

M y dog is funny
Y oung and fast and hairy

P up bites a lot
E ats everything
T erribly cheeky.

Oban Cation (7)
Kennoway Primary School, Kennoway

My Mum

M um is funny
Y ou are the best

M y mum respects me
U nderstanding, my mum is
M y mum is kind.

Ellie Blount (7)
Kennoway Primary School, Kennoway

Sister

S uper kind

I s beautiful

S uper caring

T errific

E njoys her Barbies

R eally loves pink.

Alexis Hay (7)

Kennoway Primary School, Kennoway

Best Sister

S mall
I s helpful
S uper funny
T errific
E njoys going to the neighbours
R eally nice.

Kelvin Mackenzie (7)

Kennoway Primary School, Kennoway

Mummy

M ummy is kind
U nderstanding
M um is the boss
M um is beautiful
Y ellow is her favourite colour.

Logan Simpson (7)
Kennoway Primary School, Kennoway

My Mum Is Awesome

M um is funny

U nderstanding

M y mum is amazing

M y mum is bossy

Y es, sometimes annoying.

Blake Curran (7)

Kennoway Primary School, Kennoway

The Best Mum

M y mummy is the best
U nicorns are nice
M ummy is my favourite person
M e she loves
Y ay!

Jayden Mackie (7)
Kennoway Primary School, Kennoway

Maja And Agata

S isters' eyes are cute

I love my sisters

S uper sisters

T hese sisters are awesome

E very sister is cute

R iding bikes with my sisters is good

S uper, super sisters!

Jagoda Sieklinska (7)
Kirkcaldy West Primary School, Kirkcaldy

Viktor

V iktor is his name, he's my cousin
I love him
K ind he is to me
T aking care of him is great
O nly he is good to play with
R iding bikes with him is good.

Martyna Zabek (7)

Kirkcaldy West Primary School, Kirkcaldy

Lewis

L ewis is a hero

E veryone is best friends

W hen we are with each other, we feel happy

I f we are together, we feel like heroes

S o, we like each other for all our lives.

Oliver Scott (7)

Kirkcaldy West Primary School, Kirkcaldy

Stormy

S tormy is fun

T oo cute and crazy

O nly Stormy can lick me

R uns so fast

M akes noises at night

Y esterday, he nibbled my foot.

Luka Indopoulous (7)

Kirkcaldy West Primary School, Kirkcaldy

Simba

S imba is awesome
I mpossible fun
M ad at me
B ad
A nnoying

D og is cuddly
O h so annoying
G ood.

Nikita Farmer (7)

Kirkcaldy West Primary School, Kirkcaldy

Sofia

S he is called Sofia

I love her

S he plays with me

T akes me to the park

E veryone loves Sofia

R eads to me at night.

Hope Lazmirski (7)
Kirkcaldy West Primary School, Kirkcaldy

Ziggy

Z iggy is my best friend
I give lots of treats to Ziggy
G ive him lots of snuggles
G ive him lots of walks
Y ou are very fluffy.

Elsa Venters (7)
Kirkcaldy West Primary School, Kirkcaldy

Zooey

Z ooey is the best

O h, Zooey, I love you

O opsy Zooey!

E verything for you, Zooey

Y ou're so beautiful, Zooey.

Arabella Blacklaws (7)

Kirkcaldy West Primary School, Kirkcaldy

Lewis

L ewis is an excellent friend
E verybody thinks he's cool
W izard Lewis
I like Lewis
S low Lewis.

Harvey Deacon (7)
Kirkcaldy West Primary School, Kirkcaldy

Sarah

S he is my toy dog
A very fluffy toy dog
R eally cuddly
A little bit naughty
H ungry toy dog.

Lily Meacher (7)
Kirkcaldy West Primary School, Kirkcaldy

Snowy

S nowy is cute

N ice puppy

O bedient she is

W hite and her age is two

Y outhful little pup.

Scarlett Stewart (7)
Kirkcaldy West Primary School, Kirkcaldy

Harry

H is for Harry

A is for amazing

R is for ring

R is for right

Y is for yo-yo.

Jack Fairfull (7)

Kirkcaldy West Primary School, Kirkcaldy

Toby

T oby is cute

O f course, he is super

B rilliant he is

Y ummy eating pizza.

Stephen Chaplin (7)
Kirkcaldy West Primary School, Kirkcaldy

Cody

C ute baby

O ver loveable

D otty face

Y es, I'm used to holding him.

Indie McQuade (7)

Kirkcaldy West Primary School, Kirkcaldy

Kamil

K ind
A nd mad
M ean
I like him
L ike.

Kuba Jakubaszek (7)
Kirkcaldy West Primary School, Kirkcaldy

Owen

O wen is kind
W e like to play
E nergetic
N ice.

Rory Seal (7)
Kirkcaldy West Primary School, Kirkcaldy

My Cat, Pushkin

M iaows moanily at 5am for breakfast
Y awns lazily on the cosy bed

C hases squirrels, razor-sharp claws ready
A sleep in his favourite sunny spot
T iger-striped ginger fur, soft as silk

P urrs dreamily as I tickle under his chin
U rgently runs out the cat flap to fight next door's cat
S cratches Mummy's blue velvet chair
H e hates the VET but adores his home
K eeps washing his white, wiggly, wire whiskers
I cy evil eyes stare silently upon me
N aughty... but he is the best cat in the kingdom!

Cissie Bootman (6)
Notting Hill & Ealing Junior School, Ealing

My Friends

M e and my friends we love to play

Y ou and your friends can come and say hey

F riends today, friends forever, we can all be friends

R unning as fast as zebras playing hide-and-seek

I n my school, we always play ball on the hills

E very day at home I always play with my brother

N o pushing, no spitting, we all play in peace

D oing things that are nice and helpful

S ay hello next time and don't be shy.

Jemima Omiyale (5)
Notting Hill & Ealing Junior School, Ealing

My Cat, Pishi

M y cat, Pishi, is clever
Y esterday, she caught a mouse

C heeky kitty hid it in the house
A t night she goes undercover
T iptoes to the kitchen, she's greedy!

P ishi is so soft and fluffy
I adore cuddling her even if she's muddy
S leeping is her favourite activity
H ere she comes to play with me
I love my Pishi and she loves me.

Daria Coulon (5)
Notting Hill & Ealing Junior School, Ealing

Ladybird

L aid lining up yellow tiny shiny eggs become larva

A cting like a wiggly worm stung me, "Ouch!"

D ancing aphids are eaten by naughty chubby babies

Y ellow raindrop from a pupa

B eautiful white shiny wings, the ladybird came as red as a fresh juicy cherry

"I want to fly!

R eady to meet my prince

D ance with me, let's wiggle swingy bottom. Ooh lala!"

Himari Shinno (5)

Notting Hill & Ealing Junior School, Ealing

Sisters

S ometimes I jump on the bed with Eva and Akira

I feel happy when we are all together

S o I love being one of three sisters (but sometimes wish we could be four)

T hat would mean, Papa and Mumma... *just* one more!

E xploring woodlands on our bikes is lots of fun

R ockets are cool but not as cool as my sisters

S o I try to be kind and show them how much I love them.

Ārya Sharma (6)
Notting Hill & Ealing Junior School, Ealing

My Friend, Charlotte

C is for Charlotte, my creative and cute best friend

H is for happy, how she makes me feel

A wesomely awesome is how I describe her

R is for running, she is as fast as a flash

L is for Lottie, her lovely pet name

O is for oviparous, which she is not

T is for tiny, how I feel next to her, but I know we will be

T ogether until the

E nd of time.

Eden Lily Gambling (7)

Notting Hill & Ealing Junior School, Ealing

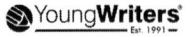

Best Friend

B uzzing with excitement
E njoy my moment with Aanya
S cented pens, I like to play with Aanya
T en number bonds, I like to play with
Aanya

F riendly and kind she is
R ise across the sky with her
I ce cream I like with her
E xplore the room with her
N icely we play together
D ancing with laughter!

Hannah Clough (6)
Notting Hill & Ealing Junior School, Ealing

My Teacher

M y teacher is very kind
R eads beautiful books
S he has lovely hair

N ever shouts at the class
I love her
C ares a lot about us
H elps me with my work
O ffers us team points
L aughs a lot
L eaves me feeling happy
S ometimes she likes to dance.

Anaahi Shah (6)
Notting Hill & Ealing Junior School, Ealing

Xinran

X ylophone makes beautiful sounds like the moonlight

I n the piano, the strings are dancing like a colourful butterfly

N othing is better than musical instruments

R ainbow is like a wonderful harp of the sun

A flute is the robin singing to the blue sky

N othing is better than nature.

Cindy Yu (6)
Notting Hill & Ealing Junior School, Ealing

Best Daddy

B oots are Dad's favourite

E very day, Dad tickles me

S ee Dad, I can see the sea

T ea is my dad's favourite

D ad likes pizza

A pples are Dad's favourite

D ads love pears

D ads love carrots

Y ay, Dad won the golf competition.

Mira Bachir (5)

Notting Hill & Ealing Junior School, Ealing

Blythe

B lythe looks cool in the rain

L ion's hair surrounds her face

Y ellow is the colour of her hair

T he deep feeling inside her is that she is funny

"H ow do cows walk on the moon?" is one of her excellent jokes

E xcitement and laughter are my best memories of her.

Umi Cook Kurihara (5)

Notting Hill & Ealing Junior School, Ealing

My Little Brother

B orn in January of this year

R ocks to sleep all the time

O ften cries as loud as thunder

T iny fingers and tiny toes

H e is my little brother whom I love and adore

E ven though he can't talk and walk

R ainbows come out when he laughs.

Yvie Huang (6)

Notting Hill & Ealing Junior School, Ealing

Alex

B est boy in the whole wide universe
R eads lots of stories with my mummy
O wns a special toy called Hedgehog
T his boy is extremely caring
H e loves his toy called Monty the Doggie
E ats lots of fish fingers
R uns around like crazy.

Isobel MacDougall (6)
Notting Hill & Ealing Junior School, Ealing

Best Friend

B eautiful ballerina

E ncouraging person

S uper strong

T houghtful friend

F earless

R eliable

I ntelligent schoolgirl

E xcellent inspiring person

N ice and neat young lady

D elightful person.

Laranya Ryatt (6)

Notting Hill & Ealing Junior School, Ealing

Cousin

C uddly Mila is such a great friend

O utstanding Zahara is always there until the end

U pbeat Mila dancing around

S weet Zahara spinning all around

I ntelligent Mila, oh so clever

N ext time I see them I will give them the biggest hug ever.

Savannah McDowell (6)

Notting Hill & Ealing Junior School, Ealing

Teacher

T oday is a sunny day

E veryone is at a cafe

A nd they all start to play

C ause it's Olivia's birthday

"H ello guys," said her mother

E verybody go into the house

R acing for the cake, let's shout hooray!

Olivia Qin (5)

Notting Hill & Ealing Junior School, Ealing

Georgia

G eorgia, Georgia, my best friend.
E legantly, she walks down the street,
O ut the door and off to school.
R adiantly, she smiles at me.
G ently, she hugs me.
I ncredibly, she sings with me.
A lways we laugh when she sees me.

Ines Coulter (6)

Notting Hill & Ealing Junior School, Ealing

Midnight

M y cat is soft

I love her

D on't wake her when she's asleep

N ight-time is nice for her

I like to stroke her

G randma says she's sweet

H er cat friend is called Snowflake

T hey like to catch mice.

Lyla Peat (6)

Notting Hill & Ealing Junior School, Ealing

Rainbow

R ay of sunshine and after the showers
A dorable as lovely flowers
I ndigo to blue to yellow to red
N ecklace of a joyful princess
B eautiful as a cheerful fairy
O h! as colourful as a butterfly
W ow! We all love rainbows!

Rishita Sharma (5)
Notting Hill & Ealing Junior School, Ealing

Brother Henry

B rother Henry is really annoying

R eally, really annoying

O n Saturdays, he likes to climb trees

T homas is his favourite engine

H e is called Henry

E ager to watch Ryan's Toy Review

R eally loves to watch Peppa Pig.

Emilia Priestley (6)
Notting Hill & Ealing Junior School, Ealing

Ariel The Mermaid

A riel is amazing at aquatics

R unning she can't do, but racing she can do

I n her cave, she inspires you by telling you interesting stories

E legantly, she swims through the water singing eloquently

L ike a fish, she is very light.

Charlotte Gilbert (6)

Notting Hill & Ealing Junior School, Ealing

Rabbity

R aisins are her favourite food

A ppels she eats in the chapel

B etter still is to hop on a hill

B eautiful she is to me

I ce cream is just for me

T ogether we want to be

Y ou are my rabbity.

Zoe Pole (6)

Notting Hill & Ealing Junior School, Ealing

My Friends

F riends are kind

R unning games are the best

I magine all the things we can do

E very day is a fun day

N ever are they dull

D ancing makes us happy

S o my friends are clever and funny.

Jasmine Takhar (6)
Notting Hill & Ealing Junior School, Ealing

Pirate

P itiless pirates with pistols
I mpatiently inspecting the inn for booty
R ampaging after the big loot
A ttacking the innkeeper
T hrilled with their triumph
E lated and escaped to the blue water.

Aadhya Parikh (6)

Notting Hill & Ealing Junior School, Ealing

Chester, My Puppy

C hester is my puppy
H e is so beautiful
E specially when he has been brushed
S ometimes he's naughty
T hough we forgive him
E very day he goes for a walk
R ound the park.

Hettie Heppenstall (6)
Notting Hill & Ealing Junior School, Ealing

My Mummy

M y mummy is very kind

U nicorns like my mummy and that matters

M ondays are her best day because I have fun

M oons are beautiful, they are like her eyes

Y ummy, my mummy sure loves eating.

Millie Milne (6)

Notting Hill & Ealing Junior School, Ealing

Mummy

M y mummy is made of elastic
U nbelievable she is, I think she's fantastic
M arvellous Mummy, she is magic
M agical Mummy, she can save me
Y ou and me love our mummies too.

Millie Lockett-Boyle (6)
Notting Hill & Ealing Junior School, Ealing

Daddy

D addy is a strong man

A nd he likes eating barbecued lamb

D riving his car makes him happy

D ancing with me makes him happier

Y ellow is not his favourite colour, green is!

Nikita Pillai (7)

Notting Hill & Ealing Junior School, Ealing

Brother

B igger than me
R eads lots of books
O f course, always telling the truth
T aekwondo champion
H andsome
E verything right
R eal because I love him.

Anika Sangwaiya (5)
Notting Hill & Ealing Junior School, Ealing

Mummy

M ummy likes to play the violin
U nder the big old tree
M ummy likes to bake a cake
M aking us happy as can be
Y ou are the best Mummy in the whole world.

Ottilie Coman (6)

Notting Hill & Ealing Junior School, Ealing

My Mummy

M y mummy is the best

U nderstanding and helpful with my homework

M e and Mummy love each other

M y mummy is lovely

Y our mummy is perfect for you.

Lubna Al-Jibouri (6)
Notting Hill & Ealing Junior School, Ealing

Grandma

G randma is giggly

R eady to help

A lways fun

N ice manners

D ines at restaurants

M otherly and kind

A nd clever.

Emma Louise Melikian (6)
Notting Hill & Ealing Junior School, Ealing

My Sister, Emily

E lephants are her favourite animal
M y brother and her argue
I ce cream is her favourite treat
L ies in her soft bed
Y es, I love her!

Josie Johnstone (5)
Notting Hill & Ealing Junior School, Ealing

My Mummy

M ornings are good and dark
U nder the sheets I'm warm
M ummy wakes me up and
M akes me a lovely breakfast
Y ummy and delicious!

Blythe Tyler (5)
Notting Hill & Ealing Junior School, Ealing

My Mummy

M agical mummy
U nder the sun she likes to play with me
M akes yummy food
M anages home and work
Y oga we love doing together.

Aanya Saboo (6)
Notting Hill & Ealing Junior School, Ealing

Koalas

K oalas are fluffy

O n their birthday they eat cake

A nd open presents

L ovely koalas are sweet

A nd I want one.

Mina Burge (5)

Notting Hill & Ealing Junior School, Ealing

Cousins

C ool boy
O ver their house
U nique friends
S uper
I like them
N ew fun games
S tar team.

Freddie Forecast (6)
Rettendon Primary School, Rettendon Common

Auntie

A mazing nurse
U nicorns are her favourite
N HS
T akes care
I love her
E veryone loves her.

Annabelle Morter (6)
Rettendon Primary School, Rettendon Common

My Mummy

M y mummy is kind
U nless I am bad
M ummy makes cakes
M e and Mummy play trains
Y es, I love Mummy.

Charlie De-Beger (5)

Rettendon Primary School, Rettendon Common

Friend

F riend, you're the best

R ight star

I love her

E njoys magnets

N ice

D aring.

Joseph Watts (6)

Rettendon Primary School, Rettendon Common

Mummy

M y mummy is kind
U pstairs to tidy
M ake-up in morning
M ummy is caring
Y ou're the best.

Ella Goodacre (5)
Rettendon Primary School, Rettendon Common

Doctor

D oes the right thing

O n call

C aring

T he nice hero

O ff comes the cast

R ocks.

Elliott Bray (5)

Rettendon Primary School, Rettendon Common

Mum

M ummy is nice to me

U sually cleaning

M akes pancakes

M ummy is friendly

Y ou are fun.

Henry Sharp (5)

Rettendon Primary School, Rettendon Common

Mummy

M um is the best

U seful Mummy

M ummy is amazing

M y friend

Y ou're the best.

Rosie Kemp (5)

Rettendon Primary School, Rettendon Common

Mummy

M ummy is strong

U seful

M ummy is kind to me

M ummy makes cakes

Y ou are lovely.

Grace Francks (5)

Rettendon Primary School, Rettendon Common

Daddy

D o your best

A mazing work

D ude with his cartwheels

D aring

Y ou are brave.

Jai Gill (5)
Rettendon Primary School, Rettendon Common

Kyle

K yle is strong
Y ou are my friend
L ikes sport
E very day he likes playing with me.

Isabelle Wang (5)
Rettendon Primary School, Rettendon Common

Mum

M agical Mum
U ses make-up
M ummy is fun
M y mummy eats
Y ou are lovely.

Macy Tinton (5)
Rettendon Primary School, Rettendon Common

Oscar

O scar is eight
S illy
C ool
A wesome
R eally nice.

Archie West (5)

Rettendon Primary School, Rettendon Common

Luke

L ikes to be cheeky

U ses my tablet

K ind of dresses up

E ats.

Beau Ayliffe (6)

Rettendon Primary School, Rettendon Common

Pet

P arrots squawk
E very day the dog barks
T he mouse is sweet.

John James Hiscott (6)

Rettendon Primary School, Rettendon Common

Ron

R uns to get vegetables

O n our laps

N ice and cuddly.

Oliver Medlock (5)
Rettendon Primary School, Rettendon Common

Dad

D ad, I love you
A mazing man
D oes great things.

Nathan McCreadie (5)
Rettendon Primary School, Rettendon Common

Carlo Ancelotti

C oach from Italy

A mazing manager

R eally hope Everton win the title

L eague title hopeful

O ld Chelsea manager.

Paul Heary (17)

The Coppice School, Bamber Bridge

Teacher

T eacher is great

E asy to talk to

A ce

C lass 5

H appy

E ntertains

R eads stories.

Lexi Coulton (12)

The Coppice School, Bamber Bridge

Harper

H appy
A lways helps Emily
R eads books
P laying
E ats mash
R uns fast.

Emily Holt (12)
The Coppice School, Bamber Bridge

Mum

M y mum makes the best food
U sually, she knows what I like
M ore and more I ask till I am full.

Josh Ormson (16)

The Coppice School, Bamber Bridge

Ruby

R eally nice sister

U nderstanding

B eautiful

Y ou are fun.

Miryam Khan (16)

The Coppice School, Bamber Bridge

Mum

M y mum likes to go shopping
U s together
M e and my mum.

Eva Hopkins (11)
The Coppice School, Bamber Bridge

Shea

S illy

H appy

E lectric

A dmirable.

Shea Hegarty (12)

The Coppice School, Bamber Bridge

Sean

S hiny
E lectric
A mazing
N osy.

Sean Nyathi (12)

The Coppice School, Bamber Bridge

Young Writers Information

We hope you have enjoyed reading this book – and that you will continue to in the coming years.

If you're a young writer who enjoys reading and creative writing, or the parent of an enthusiastic poet or story writer, do visit our website **www.youngwriters.co.uk**. Here you will find free competitions, workshops and games, as well as recommended reads, a poetry glossary and our blog. There's lots to keep budding writers motivated to write!

If you would like to order further copies of this book, or any of our other titles, then please give us a call or order via your online account.

Young Writers
Remus House
Coltsfoot Drive
Peterborough
PE2 9BF
(01733) 890066
info@youngwriters.co.uk

Join in the conversation!
Tips, news, giveaways and much more!

 YoungWritersUK    @YoungWritersCW